S E L F,
MADE

S E L F,
MADE

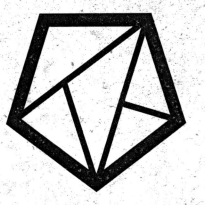

Mike Anderson

Self Made, LLC
contact@weareselfmade.com
weareselfmade.com

Ordering Information:
Quantity sales. Special discounts are available on quantity
purchases by corporations, associations, and others. For
details, contact the publisher at *sales@weareselfmade.com*.
Orders by U.S. trade bookstores and wholesalers. Please
contact *sales@weareselfmade.com*.

ISBN 978-0-9888348-6-6

Library of Congress Control Number: 2013900388

Available through the Ingram Distribution Channel
Available on the Apple App Store: "Self, Made"

Editor-In-Chief: Esther Keane - *estherkeane4@gmail.com*
Executive Producer/Cover Design: Ross Fitzgerald, President
of COMN Design • *comndesign.co*
Interior Design/Cover Layout: Frame25 Productions

Printed in the United States of America
First Edition

Table of Contents

Mom:
Thank you for pushing me and shaping me into who I am. Without you, I wouldn't believe in myself.

Uncle Phil, LD, Froni, Jason Deverna:
Thank you for being phenomenal examples of how to be a man, and helping me to become one. Without you, I would have no foundation to live on.

Ross Fitzgerald, Kevin Kelleher, Kevin Goldsmith, Jon Friedman, Joel and Esther Keane:
Thank you for all the work you put in to making this book great. Without you, it was nothing more than a dream.

Steve and Sharon Kelly:
Thank you for your leadership and wisdom. Without you, I would have no vision for my life.

God,
Thank you for everything.
Without you, nothing matters.

Acknowledgements

Graphic design/creative management:
Ross Fitzgerald, Founder of COMN Design

Editing:
Esther Keane

Promotional video for weareselfmade.com:
Kevin Kelleher, CEO and Founder of KK
Productions, www.kkproductions.co

INTRO

*"What do you want to do with
your life when you're older?"*

DAUNTING, ISN'T IT? It seems like every time I look at my Facebook feed I read a post about someone not having an answer to this question. We start to hear this question in elementary school, an age too young to fully grasp the gravity of it. We give a fantasy-driven answer. Mine, for example, was to be a quarterback for the Dallas Cowboys for the rest of my life (retirement wasn't a concept I had fully developed yet). As we grow, the question starts to hold more weight. Around middle school we begin to ponder what that day will actually look like, but then we shrug off the thought. We've got our whole lives to figure it out right? It's when we arrive to high school that the question becomes fully understood. It seems like every member of the school faculty expects us to know *exactly* what we'll be doing for the rest of our lives. And because of our own uncertainty about the topic, we ask our fellow students the same question. The thing that we don't catch is that we're all doing the same thing, everyone assuming that they are behind the curve because they don't know what they want to do with their career after high school or college.

Because of the way the question is framed, it's implied that we will only be able to reach this state of maturity *"when we're older"*. So we run into the biggest mental paradox of our young lives: Needing to be certain of our path in life years in advance, but not being able to do anything about it until an unforeseen point in the future. Are we only able to start our adult lives when we have a degree in our dream? Are we not allowed to do anything of significance while we're still young?

This question with an unlimited amount of answers becomes the most imprisoning thought in our minds: *What will I do?*

I believe that rather than being our generation's biggest burden, answering this question should be the most freeing experience of our lives. Regardless of the common opinion, you need to know that it *is* possible to know the answer to that question, and you can start doing something about it now.

My hope for this book is that the burden of that question will fall off your shoulders. My hope is that after reading this book you will not only have more clarity about your future, but also be able to take action *today.* Your age means absolutely *nothing* in regards to where you go in life, unless *you* allow it to. It's time to quit limiting ourselves, and move forward with the immeasurable amount of creativity our generation has been blessed with.

Don't let me fool you, I'm in this boat with you. While writing this book, I am currently finishing up my last year of a two year college, with no plans to pursue further education. The same question has been on my mind: What am I going to do with myself? But that question is what led me to write this book. And at this point in time, I have no idea what my next five years looks like. But I've had time to think about it, and I've begun to *plan* and *act* on what I can do. And that's what I'd like you to know, that you can start acting on your future now.

This book has three keys, points, steps, whatever cliché format you'd like. Three insights I'd like to share with you; insights that will hopefully help you discover what it is you dream about doing for a living, and how to pursue that dream *right now.* This is not a "self-help book", a "feel good book", or an "inspirational read". It's a *wakeup call.* I will not sugarcoat anything, I won't tell you how easy life will be after reading this book. Nothing written in this book means anything without your willingness to put it to action in your life. There is one thing that I can promise: you will not walk away with more questions than answers. To the best of my ability, I will lay out exactly how I believe you can start chasing your dreams now, and be successful in the venture.

FIND YOUR DREAM

LET'S GO BACK TO that heavy question for a minute: "What do you want to do with your life when you're older?" The first two words with emphasis in that loaded question are 'what' and 'want'. *What* do you *want* to do? Before we can ever begin to plan out the course of our life, we have to define *what* it is exactly that we *want* to do. Thinking about this leads to a funny little irony: we're the people who know ourselves the best, so we should be able to pinpoint what it is that we want to do. Right?

The truth is, a huge majority of us don't have any idea what we want to do. But why is that? Is it because our minds aren't "allowed" to think about such things before a certain age/maturity level? Were the generations before us afraid to take initiative at a young age? Have we been unintentionally trained to fear the thought of *the rest of our lives?*

I think there is a deeper underlying issue at hand. I believe that the reason we don't know what we want to do is because *we haven't defined it.* Think about it, have you ever taken 30 minutes to sit down and *really* think about what it is in life that makes you want to strive for more? Yeah I know, you'll have to give up an episode of your favorite show, God forbid. But isn't investing that time into your *future* more valuable than watching an awful rendition of "A Whole New World"? I promise, when you see how the investment comes back to you, you'll realize it was *well* worth it.

In order to precisely define what career path we'd like to take, we have to ask ourselves two questions.

Question 1: *What's fun?*

Think about it. Have you ever had a crappy job? My first job was at a fast food restaurant, and working there gave me a newfound love for healthy foods. While this job did help me start developing my work ethic, it was by no means a fun job for me. Personally, I don't enjoy the food industry. But, I did learn something from one of my coworkers there. He had been working at this same job for fifteen years. *Fifteen years.* That's how old I was! I was in amazement that anyone could stay in a fast food job for that long when I hated them so much. But it was when I asked him about it that my perspective was shaken. His reply to me was simple: "It's fun for me. I can't see myself being happier working any other job out there."

Let's be real. Do we really want to invest years and possibly *thousands* of dollars into studying a subject that we don't enjoy learning about or doing? Of course not, that sounds stupid when you read it on paper. Unfortunately, that's a trap that a lot of students fall into. And why is that? Because they didn't take the time to sit down and define a path that would actually bring them *happiness* while doing it. *Seeing the point?*

So having a fun job is important?

Yes. Our future success is directly tied to the love we have for our craft. Have you ever heard of a really successful surfer who hated waves? Of course not. So in order to start seeing success, we have to first find out what we love to do. Once we find that love, we can *immediately* start taking steps in the direction of how we want to see it play out in our lives.

Question 2: *Can I really see myself still doing this in the next 10 years?*

The answer to this question is crucial. It determines how legitimately interested you are in that idea. This is also the easiest way to determine if your current interest is just a phase, or a genuine potential job that you'd want to pursue. The last thing that you ever want to do is waste your time and money studying for a specific job, and then realize a year into it that you really dislike the job altogether. That's how you get caught in the trap that a lot of our parents' generation got caught in. You go to work everyday resenting what you do, but you can't quit because it's how you support yourself and your family. Forget that. Ask yourself the tough question now and save yourself the heartache.

If it's not something that you will enjoy doing for a long time, then don't do it. Now I'm not giving you permission to give up just because you're "busy". Rather, if you're going to be miserable while doing it, then it's not worth your time. I frequently find that the things I enjoy doing the most are what keeps me busy. At the end of the day, I'd rather be busy doing something I love rather than something I'm going to wake up and hate every morning.

So who is Mike Anderson, and why should you be reading this book? Don't lie to yourself, you were thinking it. And you should ask that question. Where is my credibility coming from? What have I actually done?

I'm not claiming to know every aspect of every persons' lives. I don't have a one-size-fits-all answer for every individual. I am, however, *completely confident* in what I've learned about this topic. I've experienced quite a few things, and I've observed others for a long time. With an open mind, these insights *will* help you.

Allow me to explain a piece of my story.

I arrived at Ocean Lakes High School in August 2006. I had just moved to Virginia Beach the month before, so everything was new to me. No friends, no acquaintances, nothing. My mom and dad never got married, and he lives across the country. So growing up, I definitely didn't have any natural confidence in myself. I would always have to find a new male role model, often switching from friend to friend. I found my value in how much my guy friends liked me. I never really believed I could accomplish anything worthy of recognition. If not for my mom's constant love and encouragement, I would have given up on myself. So moving to a new school, I wasn't looking forward to having to go through the whole process again. I spent my first two years of high school like this, constantly looking for approval and acceptance. If someone asked me what I wanted to do when I grew up, I felt sick to my stomach. Not only did I not believe that I could do anything worth mentioning, but I also didn't have the faintest clue of what path I wanted to take. I finished my sophomore year at Ocean Lakes, and during the summer I was invited to my church's youth summer camp. I was reluctant, but I had nothing better to do that summer, so I went.

Everything changed.

At this summer camp, my eyes were opened to the realization that I wasn't alone. People felt the same stress I did. They had the same lack of direction that I did. And not just a few fellow students, but practically *everyone.* At that camp, I realized that I was called to do everything I could to put an end to that. So during my junior year, I started an afterschool club that met once a week after school. Every week we met up and planned on how we could best get this message to our student body. We started the club with 10 people, and in 6 months we had a consistent attendance of 40 people every week. As amazing as this increase was, we were nowhere near done. In a high school with 3000 students, we had a lot more to do.

This is where I started to find my dream.

The summer going into my senior year, we planned. We put many hours into thinking, strategies, events, etc. It paid off. During my senior year, more than 300 of the school's students participated. In *one year* we went from 1.5% of our school being there to 10%. We began to make a real *difference* in our school. We took part in whatever we could to better the school and the students in it. We made a *real, positive* difference.

This is how I began to understand what my dream is. My dream turned out to be an innate desire to help people, however I could. Since then I have realized that my dream is a desire to help bring people to a place where they can see the best for their lives. This was my dream, but what is it that gets you fired up? Your love could be cars, fashion, business, music, accounting, office jobs, it really doesn't matter. What *does* matter is how you define your dream. How you define your dream will determine how you begin to act on it. So where does our dream come from?

Our dream comes from a moment of passion.

Don't get weird on me now. Let's go back to my story: my eyes were opened to a school that was afraid of how their futures would pan out, so I acted on a dream. That was a moment of *passion*. It's not just enjoying that moment, but instead sustaining that passion *even when it gets hard*. It's to *persevere* for what you love. It's not just for inspirational thoughts, it's true for every career path.

Don't believe me?

When you ask a professional snowboarder why they do what they do, they will tell you it's because of that *moment* when they carve through the fresh snow. If you ask a mechanic why they love to fix greasy cars; their reply will be because of that *moment* when they look at the inner workings of an engine. When you ask an entrepreneur why they love business, it's because of the *moment* when they think of a brilliant, innovative idea that changes society. It all comes down to a moment of "*Gosh, I love doing what I do.*"

Here's the catch: *we have to be perceptive of that moment.*

Maybe you can't think of what that is off the top of your head. That's ok. But if you want to find your dream, then widen your gaze a bit. Be perceptive of what you're doing, what you're thinking, how you're feeling. Look for the things that you see or do that seem like something you would really enjoy, and remember it. Write it down if you have to. I have a running list of things I'd like to do with my life on a whiteboard in my room. Remember, right now we're just finding it out. It is ok to have more than one thing that you like to do. This book isn't so you can pick one idea and be stuck with it forever. I want you to be able to refine the things that you love to do, so if you have to change, you can.

Now for some people, you won't have to look very hard to see what that dream is. For those people, you just have to *recognize* your *natural gifting*. Some people are just years ahead of their peers in specific areas and that makes them essentially born to do the thing they love to do.

Let's take Michael Phelps for example:

- He is 6'4", and his wingspan is 6'7".

- He has a size 14 foot.

- His hands are abnormally large.

- He is double jointed in his chest, allowing him to move more water.

- His lungs are more advanced than the average human.

The man is *built* to swim. Sometimes people are just born with natural giftings, and they should pursue the area that they've already got a headstart in, assuming that they enjoy it. If you're not one of those people, that's ok. Most of us aren't. I can honestly say that every single thing I'm good at now, whether it's a physical activity or an ability, I had no exceptional gifting in it. Everything I've learned I've had to do so through hard work and practice. And as useful as natural gifting is, if you work hard to make your own success, you will appreciate yourself more in the long run.

Now I understand that there is a group of people that can read through this chapter, even apply the principles, and still be unsure of what their interests are. Let's be real, probably the *majority* of those reading this. Here's what you need to know:

That is absolutely OK.

It's completely normal to be a junior or senior in high school and still have no idea what you want to do. It's completely normal to be a junior or senior in *college* and still have no idea what you want to do. If you've been out of college for years and still have no idea what you want to do: IT IS COMPLETELY NORMAL. If this book was directed only to those who had a clear, concrete plan for their future, then this book would never leave the bookshelf.

Even after that, I know some of you are still *overwhelmed* with pressure. You feel like you have to land on one idea, and there's dozens of different factors that add stress to the situation. You're worrying about the preparation work, the financial costs of each decision, living arrangements, how it affects your friends and family, and on top of all that you feel like you're running out of time to worry about all of this. Believe me, I *know* the feeling. I would stress myself about being stressed. But there's something I've learned that I want to share; I think it will help the process for you:

Your stress is limiting you more than the things that you're stressing about.

When all of your focus is on the stress of a situation, your mind is not capable of making a clear decision. The more stress you have while thinking about something, the less confidence you have in even *making* the decision. Here's an example:

What do you want to eat for lunch tomorrow? The possibilities are endless. You could go through the drive-through of Burger King. Or you could go home and make your own chicken salad. Or maybe it's ramen noodles and pop-tarts again. When you think about this decision, there are obviously countless possibilities. But you're not overwhelmed with the question. Why should you be? When the time comes, you're going to make the decision you want to based off of what you want.

I believe this is how you should be able to make *every* decision. When your mind is clear, you are able to see the problem from more angles, and you're able to be significantly more confident in your decision. Treating the situation as if it were an everyday choice will allow you to see every distinct factor of the issue at hand. Now is the decision of your lunch and your career on the same level? Of course not. But it gives a little perspective on how much of a fog stress can be in your life. If you want to begin making productive mental work towards finding your dream, start by working down your stress.

An idea to try is to branch out all of your potential interests on paper. Now I'm sure some of you are "too good" to do this. You're not about to do an "assignment" right? I mean really, the effort to find some paper, a pencil, and then having to sit down and *write it out?* God forbid. But if you'd like some *clarity*, then try this out. Across the top of the page, write down all of your potential ideas. Once you've gotten them down make a list next to them with all the possible pros and cons of that career path, as well as your emotions regarding each one. Once you write it out it will reveal a lot about your unspoken feelings concerning each individual path. After writing down the cons you may find out that you really don't want to pursue something down that avenue. At the same time you may find out that the pros of another area make the job a lot more enticing than you imagined it being. It never hurts to write out things to bring clarity.

If you're still undecided, that's ok. I *want* you to keep reading through the book. The points are still applicable to you, and they're definitely going to help whenever you do find that area you start gaining interest in. As long as you're making yourself perceptive to the possibilities, it's ok to take your time deciding. There's no rush. There's no deadline. This isn't an excuse to be lazy with it, but make sure you're confident in your decision before you move forward.

The truth is, you simply need to *take owner-ship* of your dream. No one else can do it for you. You *can't* ride off the coattails of someone else's dream. You *can't* truly live out a dream if it wasn't dreamt by you. You have to be the author of your own future. If you don't live your own dream, you will be *living someone else's.*

This chapter is the anchor for the rest of the book. Whatever you decide to pursue, know that you are allowed to redo this process if it doesn't work out. In fact, if you did land on your life-long career on the first attempt it would be very impressive. But in order to move forward in the book, you need to land on an idea. I'm not say-ing just come up with something just to do it, because you don't want to waste your time going through the process if the idea isn't something you'd consider spending time doing. But when you have decided on a potential idea, be confi-dent in it, and move forward.

PLAN YOUR DREAM

IF YOU HAVE THE impression that this book is a "life will come easy when you do these things" book, then this chapter will prove you wrong. This is the hardest part of the entire book. We're not just fantasizing about cool jobs anymore. We're not dreaming about the success. Right now we're going to plan it all out: how we get there, the initiative we will have to take, and the steps that will get us to our goal. We're going to be researching, digging, learning, and organizing our lives around what we want to be doing.

But first, you need to *see* it.

I'm going to challenge you to do something. If you've been reading up to this point with a lackadaisical attitude, then I need you to stop. If you continue past this paragraph with a mindset of not wanting to put in any intentional work, then it will be a complete waste of your time. Believe me, I know what it's like to have to face your future. I am in the *exact* same boat as you. But if we don't take the initiative needed to see this grow, then we're never going to see any results. But if you're ready to truly begin, then let's move forward.

You've mentally found what your current dream is. So now you can go fill out an application and hope you get lucky, right? Before you can *ever* begin to move toward your future, you have to be able to *see* yourself doing it. You need to *see* yourself achieving your dream. You need to *see* yourself being successful in this venture.

But why??

Because if you don't see your dream, you will never be able to grow your dream.

A young man named Christopher Paolini grew up in an area called Paradise Valley, Montana. As he grew he showed to be an exceptional thinker, having the most vivid imagination.

At the age of fifteen Christopher graduated from his homeschool education, leaving him to pursue whatever dream he wanted in life. So he began to write out an exceptionally intricate fantasy called *Eragon.* This story is an incredibly orchestrated tale, filled with hundreds of characters and sub-plots. For four years Christopher worked away at the story: writing, editing, revising, re-drafting. When everything was ready, he toured around the country to 135 different schools and libraries promoting his self-published book. A year later a publisher named Alfred Knopf got wind of it and decided to publish the young man's book. The epic story became a global phenomenon. Christopher Paolini became a New York Times best-selling author at the age of nineteen. Since the completion of his first book, Christopher turned his story into a four-book cycle, and has sold over 33 million copies worldwide.

Christopher *saw* his dream. Before he ever sat down at one of his book signings, he *knew* that he could be there. He believed in himself and his giftings, and he knew that if he could plan and act accordingly, he would be able to be successful.

Seeing your dream is essential. We should always have something further to reach for, something greater to be reaching for. For me, this book isn't the end of what I'd like to do. I'd love to be travelling to across the globe talking to whoever I can about these principles. And after that I'd love to start a program where young people with innovate ideas can get a foundation of knowledge to plant their idea, and a platform so they can get a jump start into their lives. We *can't afford* to not have something we're chasing after. Keep thinking of new ideas. Keep pushing.

If you don't necessarily have a natural "standout" gifting, then I would highly recommend positioning yourself around people who bring a vision out of you. For me, it's my mom and my best friends. My mom came from food stamps to a six figure job in about ten years. Between seeing that example and hearing her constant support and belief in me, I was inspired to work for better than my prior goals. All of my close friends know where I want to go with my life, and we all mutually support each other's dreams and ambitions. Ask yourself who you look up to in life, and who is supporting what you want to do. It could be your family or friends, or anyone that you look up to. It could be a teacher, a boss, or anyone who you look to as a leader in your life. Surrounding yourself with the right people who will challenge you to look ahead will significantly help you in the process of seeing your dream.

When you're able to *see* your dream, it becomes personal. Rather than just treating it like your job that gets the bills paid, you begin to treat it like your *life*. You stop perceiving it as your mundane lifestyle and start to realize that you actually have the power to shape the way your future can look. Think back to when you had all that excitement, a new idea for your life birthed in your conscious. *Run* with that excitement, let it define everything about how you work towards it.

Just by seeing.

Look ahead to that dream job. Don't just see the literal possession of it, see yourself being successful in it. Begin to see yourself making *productive and progressive advances* in your career.

Before we begin to plan out our futures, we need to also define what success means to us. The reason it's important is because of the simple philosophy of goal setting: if you have something specific to reach for, you're more likely to reach it. If you don't measure it out intentionally then you're prone to limit yourself to settling for something vague. But at the same time if you only see "success" as making six figures a year, then you may just be setting yourself up for disappointment. So how should you do it?

First, find out what a realistic goal is. What's the average lifestyle for people with that job position? You need to do the research accurately, so you can have a realistic figure to plan with. Now here's the challenge: after you've found what's realistic, make your goal a step or two *beyond* that. Don't settle for the average, strive for what's better! If you think "it's not worth my time", what do you really lose? If you're achieving your dream anyways, what waste is it for you to desire one more step forward?

There are two common misconceptions about success. The first misconception is that it's a *universal* measurement. The fact is, success is a measurement. But other people's definition is *not* always true for you. Only you can define what true success is for your life. Success is simply: Am I truly happy with my life based on my natural values?

Another common misconception is that success is only a measurement of monetary wealth. That is the furthest thing from the truth. It's so much more. As I just said, success is about whether or not you feel truly happy with your life. So that applies to *every* area of your life, not just finances. Are you happy with your family life? Your social life? Your work time/free time ratio? Do you have time to work on your personal hobbies and interests? *These* are what define success. The definition of success is not owning a Rolls Royce. The definition of success is not living on a beachfront property. Are those possibilities? Yes, but only if they line up with your personal values. Care more about your values being met than your public image of success. Cars and clothes won't bring you happiness, but the fulfillment of your innate desires for life will.

Now that you've seen it, we need to begin to plan for it.

This is the tipping point of the entire process. Either you will see the amount of prep work you have to do and quit, or you'll push through it and start to actually *do something*. If you're not ready to start planning yet, that's fine. Go back and visualize it some more, you need to make sure that this next step is undoubtedly worth it to you. It's ok to be uncertain, but don't camp here. You need to start making tough decisions, so don't waste your own time by being afraid to take the next step. Once you've made your decision, it's time to start planning.

There are a few key things that you need to intentionally plan out. To benefit yourself, you should write these down as we go along. It will help you in the long run if you see it all together.

Things you need to plan for:

You Need to Plan Your Prerequisites

Start this step as soon as possible. This is the biggest researching portion of the process, so it will take you the longest amount of time. Before you enter your dream job it would be good to know the bare minimum you have to do to get that job right? This is where you look at what your job requires educationally; whether that's a two-year or four-year degree, a technical school, special job training, an internship, previous job experience, grades, etc. This is where a lot of us get hung up, because this task can become so unbearably overwhelming. It feels even worse if you're a junior or senior because it feels like everyone is asking you about it 24/7. I know it seems like a lot, but I can promise you two things: 1) You will only continue to get more busy, and 2) You will see how unbelievably beneficial it will be for you to start this process as soon as you can. If you can knock this out early on then you can spend your later years investing time into really getting a head start on all the other inner workings of your job field.

When it comes to looking for a college, *make sure* that you are not wasting your time looking. Since you're *paying* to be there, make sure you're only looking at institutions that have the classes you're looking for, and have capable teachers to teach you everything you need to know.

Use the resources available to you! Ask your parents or teachers for help. Guidance counselors literally get paid to help you with these kind of decisions, so make them earn their salary! Go to college seminars, go to the big conventions where you can meet their representatives. Take campus tours, go to the information sessions. Will you lose some free weekends? Of course. But will you be significantly more prepared for life than the people who didn't? Undoubtedly.

During this process, *make sure* that you're researching if you have to partake in any internships to do your job. I've heard countless horror stories of people spending years in schools not realizing that they had to complete a mandatory internship before they could ever pursue that career. Again, don't waste your own time. Do a quick Google search in advance and make the process a lot less painful.

This next thought can be very easily misinterpreted, so hear me out: I do not think that EVERYONE needs to/should go to college. I will say that this is a *very* rare occasion, but it does exist. For example, if your dream is to be a musician, and you believe that you can be successful doing so, then GO FOR IT. Don't let anyone's ignorant "college or failure" opinion prevent you from chasing your dream. Now with that, be a little realistic. If you're in a band with your friends and the only show you've played is in front of your parents in your garage, maybe you should take some time to consider something a little more lucrative. But if you/your band are good at what you do then by all means go out and work for it. I know quite a few people in the music scene in Virginia and it is definitely not the easy life people assume it to be. People who want to make a career out of music have to *hustle*. With buying equipment, practicing sets, taking voice/instrument lessons, writing songs, learning covers, booking shows, distributing music, building a fan base, self-marketing, and learning how to network, *all* while working a full-time job to support yourself; musicians have their work cut out for them. But if you think that you can skip college and be a lawyer, you need to get your head straight.

If you're in the category who is still unsure of what area to pursue, you can still be preparing for prerequisites. If you think further education is in your future then getting your general education classes out of the way would be a resourceful thing to do. This is also a beneficial way to start seeing more potential career choices, because you'll be able to take a wide variety of elective courses. If you don't think college is in your future, then try working a job or two in the areas that have a potential lead in your interests. The best way for you find out if you will enjoy doing something is to put yourself in that environment.

So put yourself in a position where you can see the day-to-day of your potential career.

Again, don't let your uncertainty prevent you from applying these thoughts. Later on I'm going to share a story with you about a young man named Joel and how he's been living his life while being undecided about the next step for his future.

Make sure you take your time in this section, because that will be the last thing you want to go back and have to do again. Write the list of objectives down as you go, or type it up and save it. Once you see a tangible checklist in front of you, accomplishing the individual goals will be much easier to manage.

You Need to Plan Your *Timing*

Timing is *crucial.* Without beneficial timing, you will significantly limit the amount you're able to accomplish in the time you're working. For a very blunt example, if you wait until you're thirty-five to decide you want to follow your dream to be a starting college quarterback, odds are you missed your physical prime. Intentional timing is what almost all multi-millionaires have in common. They started doing what they loved when they were our age. I'm not saying they were playing the stocks at sixteen, but they were at least taking the steps to learn what they needed to.

You have to be intentional about your timing. You can let events happen to you as the world dictates, but again, you'll be wasting more of your time. If you grab a spirit of intentionality and start making events happen when *you* want them to, you will see that a lot of efficiency and effectiveness will follow you. If anything, you want to be able to control how your life is decided, rather than depending on other people's timing to dictate your life.

The best example I can give of a company that has perfected intentional timing is Nike. Their strategy when it comes to releasing shoes is unequivocally the most brilliant marketing work ever done by a company. Need proof? Think about how after every winter holiday break you hear rumors in the school about how people waited outside of a shoe store for *hours* just to buy a pair of shoes. And you see on the news how there were fights breaking out, stores broken into, robberies, and even murders over individual pairs of Jordans. Or even in 2011, when Nike released a shoe dubbed the Galaxy Foamposite.

This shoe was unbelievably limited in volume, so people camped out for weeks. In Florida, some of their major cities had Police and SWAT teams stationed at shopping malls to control riots...for a shoe! This is publicity that money cannot buy. By no means am I saying that Nike is trying to cause riots, robberies, or murders. But I am saying that their ability to create a culture that has a devoted fanbase is unrivaled. We need the same kind of intentionality in our personal and professional lives. If we want to see real effective success, then we have to start working towards being intentional with our timing.

You Need to Plan Your *Obstacles*

We live in a generation where we have access to an unquantifiable amount of information at the click of a mouse, and yet we use that freedom to watch Rebecca Black 167 million times. Every other minute there's a tweet posted about a success story sharing their advice on what not to do when coming up through their industry. Yet for some reason we assume that that's only for the adults currently going through that season of life. Then we miss the warning and fall into the *exact same* trap that had just been posted on Twitter.

Take a step back and look at it, does that not frustrate you? I hate wasting time by making a mistake that I could have easily prevented by seeing how people before me handled it.

The truth is, we *are* going to have obstacles in our path. Everyone does. But if we can learn what's going to come up ahead of time, then we can make adjustments and plan to get through it with the least amount of resisitance.

You Need to Plan Your *Successes*

We have such a weird viewpoint when it comes to this topic. We work hard in the area that we want to be successful, but if someone tells us to plan out how and when we're going to be successful we find it uncomfortable. Why? Being comfortable with your successes is being confident in your abilities and knowing that you'll be able to use them successfully. If you're *not* confident enough in what you're doing to be able to plan out your successes, then you *shouldn't* be working towards them.

It's not a matter of self-esteem, it's a matter of goal-setting.

Goal-setting is one of the most effective methods to accomplishing tasks. If you want to be a basketball player, you'll set mental benchmarks to mark your success while you play. If you want to be a journalist, you'll set mental benchmarks of where and when you get published to mark your success while you write. We all do it naturally. Our challenge is to put it down on paper ahead of time. When we *intentionally* do it, we have to face the fear that we might not meet them.

Let that fear motivate you to strive for success.

Here's something you *need* to know. You CANNOT sustain overnight success. Please, don't chase after the lifestyles of people who appear to have it all together because they have money to buy whatever they want. Would it be fun to be a reality tv celebrity for a few years? Sure. Would it be fun to make $5000 to walk in a club and party for a few hours? Sure. But, is it going to be fun if your fame doesn't outlast you? What happens when the show stops airing? If they don't have something to transition to after their fifteen minutes of fame then what will their future really look like? Here's the truth behind those kind of situations:

If you bank on being an overnight success, you can bank on being an overnight flop.

Lasting success comes through diligence and hard work. There is no substitute.

The last thought about planning is just that: there is no substitute. You can let things happen or you can lazily plan, but in the end the results will show for themselves.

What do I do in the meantime?

So you've done some planning and you like everything you've written down, but there's still a period of time where you can't do anything about it. Maybe you're in middle school or early high school and there's nothing you can do yet to get internships or related jobs. Or maybe you've graduated already and haven't been moving in the right direction so far, and even though you want to there's still some time before you can actually do anything towards it. Here's my personal recommendation:

Take a job that supports one of your hobbies.

I'll give you an example. I am a *sneakerhead*. I absolutely indulge myself in the shoe world. Jordans, Kobes, Lebrons, Foamposites: they're all my weakness. I follow sneaker blogs on a daily basis and I even have had my own sneaker-driven article I write periodically. Give me a hot sneaker, make it a little hard to acquire, and I'll fall in love. To some people it's a completely unnecessary commodity, but to me it's a lifestyle.

Back to the point. When I started my two year college program I knew that I wasn't going to be living out my dream job while I was in college, and I would still need a job. I knew without a doubt that whatever I picked wouldn't be long term, it would just be something to do while I was in this season of life. So I decided to pick a job that I knew I would really enjoy doing because it was filled with something I loved: I got a job at Foot Locker.

Is there some deep thought inside that point? Not at all. And it's not the only course of action for you to take. There are plenty of other things to consider when looking for a job; I'm just a firm believer that you should enjoy what you get paid to do. Also, if you're still unsure as to what you want to do in your future, getting jobs in things you like to do can be a good way to expand your horizons. Working at a fast food restaurant might make you realize that you love that lifestyle and that you want to manage your own branch, or even start your own chain of fast food restaurants. Working a job that you love to do is a great way to start refining your dream.

You Need to Plan for the *Unexpected*

If I've learned anything about planning in my life, it is that things almost never go the way I map them out. That's the thing about life; there is always going to be things that will be different from how you imagined them. A perfect example is this point being in my book. My original plan was to graduate from my two year college and immediately go into the process of publishing this book. Well, life happened differently. Things got pushed back, more time was needed to make things better, so I had to get a full time job in the meantime. This was a *huge* change for my daily routine. You have to understand, for the past two years I had been working jobs with no more than 20 hours a week, and all of a sudden I need to get a full time job. After applying at a few different places, I landed a job at Movement Mortgage as a loan processor. Granted, the work environment there has been intentionally set up to be the most efficient and motivating career ever made. I couldn't ask for better from Corporate America. That being said, my dream job is not to be a loan processor . . . but this brings me to my next thought:

You have to be willing to do something you may not be excited about during transition.

Sometimes, it is completely necessary to have a transitional job. And often times, those jobs aren't something we really have any emotional or mental attachment to. For me, I had to pick up a job and go through multiple weeks of training, the whole while knowing that I wasn't going to work here in a few years. But it was *necessary.* If I wasn't able to do that, then I know that I'd never be able to get where I have with this book. Don't get discouraged if you have to take a job during the in-between seasons in your life.

RECAP:

Things you need to plan for:

- You need to plan your *prerequisites.*

- You need to plan your *timing.*

- You need to plan your *obstacles.*

- You need to plan your *successes.*

- You need to plan for the *unexpected.*

In order to see the BEST for your life you need to *understand* why planning is so important. Because you *will* be using it for the rest of your life.

LIVE
YOUR
DREAM

AT THIS POINT WE'VE thought about our dream, we've developed a vision for where we want to take it, and we've done all the planning we can do. Right before you are living your dream out there's one thing you have to do: *Take the step.*

It sounds pretty easy but this is where most people quit the journey. They spend time and money preparing for their lifelong dream job and then when it comes time to finally make the move, they freeze with fear. Unable to take the initiative to make the decision they throw it away and settle for a job that they *tolerate* rather than *enjoy.* They then wonder what could have been if they would have been courageous.

I can't emphasize enough how important it is to be *confident* in your decision. Don't allow the uncertainty of change to alter the course of your life. You already *know* that this is what you want to do, you've done all the research. You've made all the plans. If it turns out to not be your fit, that's ok. You still know how to find out what will be right for you. Just don't let the fear of making the wrong decision prevent you from making any decision.

Secondly, you need to understand that hard work *will* be involved. Decide early on if it's worth the workload, because that's the one thing that won't change about your job. The requirements to get there will be the same, there's not a shortcut to the life you want. If it's worth having, then it's worth putting in the work for.

On September 1st, 2010 Justin Bieber performed his first concert at Madison Square Garden. He sold out the most coveted venue in America in 22 minutes. Regardless of whether or not you're a fan of his music it is undeniable that this is a benchmark of success for his career. It can become very easy for us to enviously desire that level of success. Everyone can see his fame now. And because we can we desire to have success comparable to that *now*, without thinking of the work needed to put into it. Everyone sees Justin's life now. But nobody saw the *decade* of work he put into it when no one was watching. His entire young life he performed shows for people and continued to get better. My favorite quality about Justin is that he didn't let his age define when he would act on his dreams. He knew what he desired in life and he took initiative to act on it as soon and often as he could. The few years of his success that we've seen was preceded by almost a *dozen* worth of preparation. That is the best representation of pushing through the hard work to achieve your dreams. If you want to really see your goals achieved, then be prepared to work for them.

I'd like to use individuals' stories to give you some thoughts on *what to keep in mind while living your dream*. All of these people are currently in the *exact* same position as you and I. As I interviewed them it became clear that each of their stories had sound insight to keep in mind while going through your journey. Enjoy the elongated story time.

Ross Fitzgerald

Ross Fitzgerald is a 19 year old African-American man. (Political correctness can make any sentence sound ridiculously lame.) He is currently a freelance graphic designer, producer, and rapper. He is finishing up his high school education through a homeschooling program and has no plan of pursuing further education. But honestly, as one of his good friends, I can say that he really doesn't need to. Ross is *exceptionally* gifted in *many* areas, all of which can make him very successful. His mind was *made* to excel in creative fields, and that's how his story starts.

Ross's creative journey began with music. He was first introduced to music when his elementary school made him learn how to play the recorder (didn't we all?). He soon moved on to play the cello, which he played for approximately one year. It was while playing the cello that he *really* fell in love with music and the ability to create it. After seeing the movie "Drumline" Ross was inspired to join his highschool's drumline team (didn't we all?). During this musical season he learned the rhythmic patterns of percussion. In his 8th grade year he saw a commercial on MTV for the production program called "FruityLoops", and decided that he wanted to give music production a try. So he started to make beats. Ross will be the first to admit that his first few beats were awful. But he knew he had a genuine interest in it and that if he kept working at it he could improve.

Just when his life felt comfortable, his situations turned. Through a series of poor choices Ross was kicked out of his high school during his freshman year. Common opinions would tell Ross that his life couldn't be anywhere near as fulfilling as his high-school graduate counterparts. People would say that he wouldn't make as much, never be able to do as much, and never be as successful.

But Ross didn't give into the *common* opinion. Instead, he made the best of his situation. He knew what he aspired to do in the future so he decided to invest his newfound time into perfecting all the crafts that he had taken an interest in. He spent countless hours learning how to craft new sounds and write lyrics. He even decided to learn new abilities such as graphic designing and entrepreneurship. Rather than let his negative circumstance define him, he chose to attack his dreams with an unwavering vigor. At age sixteen he started a rap group called "Def Beach Society". Since their founding Ross has produced three mixtapes and one e.p. for the group, as well as designed all the cover art and single track art. If that weren't enough initiative, at age seventeen Ross launched his first business: a clothing company called "Dawson." And if *that* weren't enough, in early 2012 he started his first graphic design company: COMN Design Co. His design skills were so far beyond his years that he got his first request to help design a book the same year... can you guess which one? Ross's plan for his future is to have a major hand in all of these areas, and to leave his mark on their respective cultures.

Ross's life story screams one thing:

Your dreams are worth fighting for.

The truth is, we all go through things that hinder us achieving our success. Even in the midst of being successful, problems are *bound* to arise. But if you're wholly committed to your dream, fight to keep it!

William Paul Young wrote a book called *The Shack.* He sent his book to countless publishers, but all rejected him. But he knew this was his dream, and if he wanted to see it succeed he would have to fight for it. So he did. After setting up his book through self-publishing he went on to sell over 20 million copies. William fought for his dream, despite negativity.

Your willingness to fight through negative circumstances will show you how much you really want to be where you're at. DO NOT give up just because the battle gets hard. Take every opportunity you can to grow and learn more about what you're doing. If you're going to commit the time to plan and prepare for your life, *please* be willing to fight for it when the occasion arises.

Kevin Goldsmith

Our next story belongs to Kevin Goldsmith. He represents the majority of graduating high school students in that he is immediately going to college and starting his career after getting his degree. His particular interest in life happens to be the finer arts of culinary. In March 2012 he will have started the Associate's program at the Culinary Institute of America in New York. This is his story:

Kevin's culinary interest started in fifth grade. He spent a lot of time around his uncle who was the head chef at a local crab shack. He always had a natural interest in the intricacies of how his uncle would prepare meals but he never really explored his love for cooking until he moved to Virginia Beach, VA to attend Ocean Lakes High School. For his class requirements he had to take an elective and the only one that seemed even remotely appealing to him was "Occupational Foods". Over the course of the year Kevin naturally excelled in the class, with everything coming to him with relative ease. His teacher noticed that he had promise, so she decided to invite him to do a catering event with her. At this point Kevin's mind for cooking was stirred, but he wasn't fully committed to the idea of making it a lifelong career.

During his sophomore year he wasn't able to take any cooking classes because of the grade level requirements on each class. So he took the year to practice cooking what he could at home. When his junior year began be decided to enroll in the school's program with Votech: a local technical school. He spent the first half of every day at Ocean Lakes taking required classes, then the second half would be spent at Votech learning the culinary arts. During this year of training he learned how to cook a number of basic dishes. It was through this process that he realized that this was his dream. "After all the work was done we would be standing around eating the dishes we had made. And it was during these moments that I truly understood that I really *enjoy* what I'm doing. I knew that I wanted to experience this for the rest of my life."

It was after this realization that Kevin started to *plan* his dream out. After he took some time to intentionally plan, he had a five year plan laid out for himself.

During the summer of his junior year, Kevin realized that he only needed three general education credits to graduate from Ocean Lakes. After a lot of thought and conversation, Kevin decided to take his classes over the summer and graduate high school early. For Kevin, he realized that he absolutely *knew* what he wanted to do with his life, so another year at high school wouldn't have benefitted him in regards to pursuing his career.

Because he wanted to pursue a culinary career he knew from his planning that he would have to start getting some job experience under his belt. Kevin began to apply for line cook and prep cook positions all across town but because he was only sixteen, he was rejected from a dozen or more restaurants. Knowing that he couldn't just give up, he decided to apply to the next best thing to a restaurant: Chickfila. Wanting as much experience as he could get he worked 40+ hours a week, all while finishing up his last few high school classes at home.

After several months, Kevin's diligence finally paid off. With the help of a friend, he got a line cook job at "Back Bay Gourmet," a local Mediterranean bistro. Kevin worked here for some time, learning everything he could about cooking and the restaurant business. Kevin sewed his time, and worked diligently to better his trade.

After months of hard work Kevin decided it was time to take the next step towards his dream. On March 26th, 2012, Kevin started the first day of his Associate's degree at the Culinary Institute of America at the age of *seventeen*. His plan after he graduates is to start his first restaurant and build it up to a place of independence. Once it's become stable his vision is to eventually start his own five-star restaurant.

Ever since Kevin realized what his dream was, there only was one thing on his mind:

Committing to your dream isn't an act, it's a process.

He applied to twelve different restaurants and was rejected from every single one. Let's be honest, how many of us can say that after a dozen rejections we wouldn't consider giving up that job? But Kevin pushed through the rejection, because he knew that if he really wanted the future he had planned for he would have to start somewhere. Even while he was working a full-time job he was still finishing up his classes to graduate high school. All for one reason: so he could pursue the dream he wanted to. It is so crucial for us to realize that being *committed* to our dream isn't just an event that happens when we define or plan it out. Being truly *committed* to our dream never really ends. We have to make the decision to commit every day, or else we'll wind up settling for something less than ideal.

Esther & Joel

Our next story is about two siblings: Esther and Joel. Being in the same immediate family they are both going through the same situations in life. The difference in their stories is the way they're individually handling what they want to do with their lives. We'll start by telling Esther's story.

Esther grew up as a pretty normal teenager. Coming up through high school she had average grades, and absolutely no idea what she wanted to do after she graduated. She had the worst possible case of senioritis: she didn't apply to any colleges, she failed her SAT, and she had no backup plan to fall on. When she didn't have any other choice she went to her local community college to try and figure out what she wanted to do. She spent one year there, and was unable to pass her first math class after two attempts so she dropped out.

"I was living my day to day life feeling defeated. I had zero sense of accomplishment. I kept feeling like I would be stuck in this holding pattern forever." Esther's life resembles where a lot of us are at now: we feel pressured to make a decision, but we feel we are unable to.

Esther's first step towards change came after a challenge from someone she looked up to. They challenged Esther and many others to develop a vision for their lives. Esther *really* grabbed ahold of those words. She realized that what she needed was a foundation of discipline in her life. So she decided to enroll in a two year leadership college. This isn't a typical college; it's one that's built to challenge people to expand their capacities by putting them in positions where they have no other choice but to grow. So she went through the two year program, and by the end of it was ready to move on to bigger things.

After a creative writing assignment towards the end of her second year, Esther realized that her unrecognized passion in life was her love for writing. She had always had a *huge* passion for reading and writing, and she realized that would be something that she could see herself doing full time. So the next logical step for her would be to go back to public education.

The thought of this next step *terrified* Esther. She had such bad experiences with school in the past, how would she be able to get through four more years of schooling? But because she knew what she wanted to do, she took the risk and started to chase her dreams.

Esther chose her major to be English Literature, which fit in perfect with what she wants to do. Going through her bachelor's degree people constantly criticized her for what she decided to major in. They said that a degree like that wouldn't lead anywhere. But she knew what her vision was, and she stuck to it, regardless of what she heard.

It was during her junior year when Esther took a "Creative Writing" class. During this class they had periodic assignments where they all had to write papers and then critique a paper from someone in the class. Esther found that she *loved* doing this almost as much as writing. She had never considered being an editor before but because she discovered it through doing what she wanted to do she was interested in seeing where it could take her.

Esther's life currently consists of applying for internships as an editor and submitting her writing to different publications. Her dream job isn't one that comes easily so she's putting in the hard work to make it a reality for herself. She's taking on editing projects to keep building her professional resume. In fact, one of her editing projects is helping to edit this book.

Joel's story is much simpler, but I believe he will relate to the majority of people reading this book. Joel is currently in the same leadership college that his sister graduated from, because he envied the change that he saw in her life after going through it. But unlike Esther, Joel has no idea what his next five years will look like. He's not sure if he wants to pursue more college. He's not sure if he wants to start working. He's not even sure what job he's interested in starting first. But he does know one thing: he will *boldly* make each decision when it comes time to. He may not know exactly what it is that he wants to do next, but he knows that he will be able to make a confident decision when the time comes.

I initially interviewed Joel in early 2011. Since then, things have changed in his life. Using the process discussed in this book, he found that he really has a passion for the film industry. So he planned out everything: his prerequisites, the timing, the obstacles that could be in his way, his potential successes, and the unexpected. From that he found that the next step he needed to take to pursue his dream was to enroll himself in a technical college that would allow him to focus on creative arts. Now he is focused and determined to make the most out of himself.

Esther and Joel's lives went through many changes and challenges. Between college classes and career choices, things never went according to plan. But they both decided early on that...

You have to be ok with change.

Change is *inevitable*. For every five plans I make for my life, six changes take place. The *only* thing that is unchanging in life is things *will change*. What you have to realize while living out your dream is that things are typically not going to go according to plan. The biggest advantage you can give yourself is being prepared to *adapt* to whatever changes come your way. If you know in advance that changes are going to come, then prepare yourself incase change comes. Plan it out as if everything was up to you, but live ready to change everything at a moment's notice.

RECAP:

Things to remember while living your dream:

• **Your dreams are worth fighting for.**

• **Committing to your dream isn't an act, it's a process.**

• **You have to be ok with change.**

If you want your dream to be long-term then do your best to manage these three areas. If you don't keep an intentional hold over the maintenance of your dream, then it has a chance to slip out from under your grasp. Write these points down and put them somewhere you will see every day so you can constantly be reminded that your constantly changing process of a dream is worth fighting for.

What more could he have to say after telling me to live my dream? We're not going to stop with just acquiring your dream. Because the truth is, there is something so much more fulfilling if you will only take some extra initiative. There's more to acquire at hand. This thought is extra-credit, but as we all know from final exams, taking advantage of extra credit is *well worth it.*

I want you to be able to INNOVATE your dream.

This part is for the risk-takers, the visionaries, the dreamers, people unafraid to strive for more. *Oh, well that doesn't sound like me.* It is you. This is not for "elite" people. This is for *everyone* reading this book. If your dream is secure, then the only thing stopping you from taking it a step further is *taking that step!*

The definition of innovation is the act of introducing something new. Everyone that's accomplished something worthy of recognition has done it by doing something *new*. Now I understand, we can get anxious when we think about having to start something new. New means risk, and risk means that there's a chance to fail. Risk means a chance of rejection. What if we fail?

What you *need* to know is that the failure of one risk *does not* guarantee the failure of more.

Walt Disney was fired as a young man from a newspaper editor because "he lacked imagination and had no good ideas". He also started many businesses, but failed and ended up bankrupt. Today, the Disney Corporation's market value is estimated around 57 billion dollars.

Michael Jordan was cut from his high school basketball team. He went on to win SIX rings, and build the biggest shoe brand ever based around a single athlete. When Nike signed Michael, they took a risk that they thought would make their company better. They expected to hit three million dollars in Jordan's sneakers sales between the third and fourth year. Because they took the risk, they hit 130 million in the first year.

Bill Gates dropped out of Harvard University. He also started started a business called Traf-O-Data, which failed. Today, his personal net worth is estimated around 61 billion dollars. Microsoft is valued around 230 billion dollars.

Failure is all but guaranteed. *Don't let that discourage you.* If you push through the fear of failing, you'll be able to accomplish something significant. Don't view it as anything more than a learning experience.

The main question you need to ask yourself when innovating your dream is "How can I make this better?" That's it. Take your dream and *push it farther.* See how far you can take it. Why not see if you can be the *best* in your industry? Why not see if you can make history in your field?

STRIVE for your dream.

SELF
MADE

So why the title "Self, Made"?

The fact is, all of these points can inspire you if you want them to. They can offer you really good advice, you can write them down, you can even talk about them. You tell people about your dream, and you can even have friends and family completely supporting you. You can memorize everything this book has to say.

But if YOU *don't take the step to put it to use, then it's all worthless.*

It all comes down to you. Some of you may find that sentence to be a little intimidating. You might feel pressure from having to actually make a decision. Let me show you something:

- Because it comes down to *you*, *you* get to decide what *you* want to do.

- Because it comes down to *you*, you're not living out anyone else's dream.

- Because it comes down to *you*, *you* can define what success is for *your* life, rather than letting someone else define it for you.

Don't give up this journey. If you don't find your perfect job the first time around, *try again*. I want you to know that you *can* do this. If you will put in the effort, and believe in your dream, then there's no limit to what you're going to be able to do. Find it, plan it, and live it. Innovate it. Be confident in your life. Your future is important. Not just to you, but for everyone around you. Be bold. Be steadfast. Be proactive.

You *will* achieve
your dream.

About the Author

MIKE ANDERSON is an observer.

He has observed society for twenty years.

He has seen a standard develop that he is not willing to accept.

His drive will not allow him to sit idle.

This book is the tangible result of his desire to make a change.

There is more to come.

Twitter: Mike_VA_

Instagram: Michael_Anderson

Follow the Movement: *Twitter* - selfmade

The branding for this product
was handled by Comn Design Co.

Let us brand your dream.
COMNDesign.co

CPSIA information can be obtained at www.ICGtesting.com
Printed in the USA
BVOW071144270113

311619BV00002B/23/P